STONEHENGE:

The Dragon Path and the Goddess

The story of earth magic,
Mother Goddess worship
and sacred marriage

Romy Wyeth

Illustrations by Brian Lewis

GEMINI

First published by Gemini, Chitterne Road, Codford, Wiltshire, BA12 0PG

© 2000 Romy Wyeth and Brian Lewis

Design and typesetting by Ex Libris Press, Bradford on Avon

Printed and bound by Shires Press, Trowbridge

ISBN 0 9515199 5 6

CONTENTS

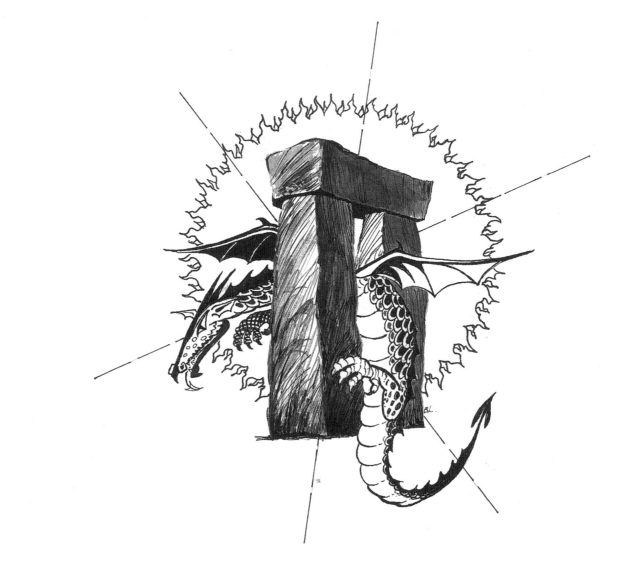

Introduction

Long before the birth of Jesus Christ the Chinese recognised the existence of a form of earth energy which they called the Dragon Power. The lines of energy ran throughout the planet carrying the life force in the same way that veins carry blood around the human body, these lines were known as the Dragon Paths.

The peoples at the dawn of history – the Sumerians, Egyptians, Hittites, Phoenicians and Scandinavians – had the Mother Goddess/Earth Mother as a focal point of their worship. She was the giver of life and her fertility ensured their survival. The Sky God, the Sun, was the deity whose union with the Goddess resulted in the fertility of the crops and the herds. From the sky came the heat and the rain, which fertilised the seeds from deep within the fecund earth. For the early farmers the mating of the Gods would have been an integral part of their existence.

At Stonehenge the Dragon Paths and the Way of the Goddess meet. The great pagan temple on Salisbury Plain in Wiltshire is the most mysterious and magical of the Bronze Age stone circles. This is the story of the Goddess and the Dragon, of sacred marriage and of earth magic.

The Way of the Goddess

Genesis

Stonehenge was constructed over a period of 1,500 years. The first stage of building began in the middle of the Neolithic Age, around 3,000BC, an earthwork consisting of bank and ditch enclosure, a henge monument that probably took up to fifty years to complete. There were various terminals where the deposits of animal bones, including the jawbones of oxen, were deliberately placed, but the main entrance poited towards the direction of the midsummer sunrise.

Inside the circular henge bank the builders dug a series of fifty-six pits, known as the Aubrey Holes after John Aubrey, the antiquarian who discovered them while surveying the monument for King Charles II in 1666. The pits may have held upright posts and one theory as to their purpose is that the henge bank may have made a false horizon, and that it was possible to make a calendar by charting the movements of the sun and the moon using the posts in the Aubrey Holes as calculation markers. At a later date cremation burials were introduced into the pits.

Beneath the topsoil of the Plain is white chalk rock, the limestone formed by the bodies of sea creatures that lived during the Cretaceous period. Stonehenge stands on a landscape made up from the bodies of marine organisms that died at least 65 million years ago. This was the last age of the dragons, when the dinosaurs and giant reptiles walked the earth. The mild climate with its seasonal variations encouraged the growth of deciduous trees and flowering plants. It was the time when the rocks of the Andes and the Rocky Mountains were forming.

When the henge was first built the chalk bank would have been exposed, the circular enclosure, gleaming white against the green vegetation of the Plain, would be clearly visible from great distances. The site lies as if at the

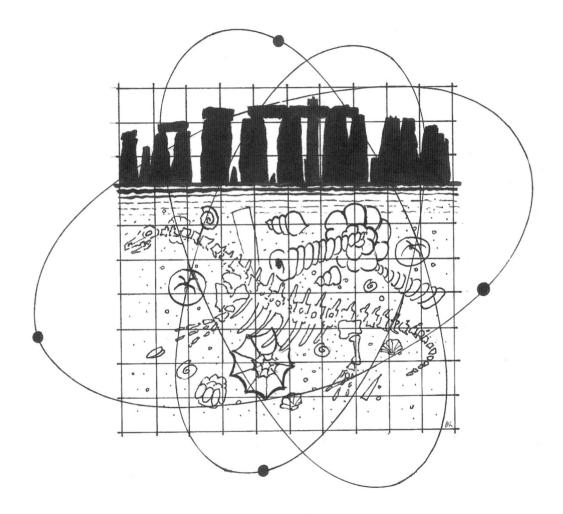

bottom of a saucer, first glimpsed from the saucer's rim. When viewing the heavens from the sacred site the curve of the earth is very obvious. The henge bank was more than six feet, above the head height of the people. From inside the chalk circle the horizon would have been level and much closer, the curve of the earth more pronounced. On a starry night with the light of the moon and the stars reflecting off the chalk, it must have looked as if the heavens were cradled in the cupped palms of the earth.

The Cosmic Consummation

To the north, just out of view of the henge is another earthwork monument, the Cursus, consisting of two parallel banks almost two miles long. Dr. Julie Gardiner of Wessex Archaeology believes the Cursus was built to be viewed and used along its length. The Cursus is contemporary with the henge bank, approximately 3,000BC, and its purpose is unknown. It was some kind of ritual enclosure, a sacred space, and may have been used for ceremonial processions or funeral games to honour the dead.

In his book, *Stonehenge: The Secret of the Solstice,* Dr Terence Meaden says this could have been where cosmic consummation of the Gods was seen to take place. Dr Meaden is a physicist and atmospheric meteorologist who founded the Tornado and Storm Research Organisation and edits the *International Journal of Meteorology.* He specialises in the study of atmospheric vortices, tornados, whirlwinds, waterspouts and ball lightning,

Dr Meaden believes that 5,000 years ago a small tornado tore up earth and trees along what was to become the route of the Cursus. The Neolithic farmers, seeing the funnel of air connect with the earth, believed the phallus of the Sky God had entered the Earth Mother, that they had witnessed the marriage of the Gods. They may have built their monument to represent the vagina of the Mother Goddess, penetrated and exposed by the Sky God, the Cursus monument commemorating this

sacred act of cosmic consummation.

The British Valley of the Kings

The landscape around the monument is sacred – the Valley of the Kings of pre-history. The highest concentration in Britain of burial mounds, Neolithic long barrows and Bronze Age round barrows can be found within three miles of Stonehenge. The barrows or tumuli contain the bodies of the leaders of society: tribal chieftains, warriors and priests. Some of the barrows contained women's bodies, indicating that women had status within the prehistoric communities of the Plain.

The barrows were tribal centres of the sacred mysteries, celebrating the life cycle of birth, death and reincarnation. Bodies were exposed, sometimes within enclosures or on wooden platforms to protect them from scavenging animals, until decomposition was complete. On occasion fleshed bodies were placed in the mounds, usually laying on their sides or sitting against the wall with their knees under their chins. Ancestor worship,

utilising parts of the skeleton for ceremonies, was common. Once the bodies were disarticulated, skulls and bones were taken from the mounds, to be used in the mystic rituals. It was unimportant that they were returned to their original position when their function was complete. The Neolithic long barrows were multiple burial places for the most important members of the tribe – men, women and children buried together, perhaps in family groups.

In the Bronze Age smaller round barrows, individual burial mounds containing grave goods such as weapons, tools, jewellery and pottery, replaced the long barrows. In death the people returned to the earth, their burial mounds reminiscent of the pregnant womb of the Goddess. Two methods of burial were used. If they were cremated the earthenware pots were frequently placed so that the unsealed opening was facing downwards, perhaps so that their ashes could mingle with the Earth Goddess who had given them life. Inhumations were in the crouched or the foetal position. They were returning to the womb in the birthing position, to make it easy for the Goddess to bring them forth when they were reincarnated.

If the barrows were chambered tombs the entrance was likely to be aligned towards an important sunrise. The sun's rays would infiltrate the entrance, illuminating the passageway into the furthermost part of the mound, where the chambers were. The Sky God was mating with the Earth Mother, penetrating the vagina [the passage] into the sheltering uterus, impregnating the Goddess, perhaps quickening the dead for the time of rebirth.

The Welsh Bluestones Around 2,400BC the Beaker People, so called because among their grave goods were beakers, pottery drinking vessels without handles, began to build the monument that would outlast civilisations. The first stones to arrive were the Bluestones – volcanic rocks, mainly spotted diorite – which weighed up to four tonnes. The source of the Bluestones was the Preseli Mountains in South Wales. Recent research by Wessex Archaeology has established the stones came from ten different sites within a few miles of each other.

The Beaker People are thought to have come to Britain from the Rhineland area of Germany. Their journeying would have taken them through the Preseli Mountains as they prospected for gold, copper and tin, travelling widely across south-west England and into Ireland.

The Preseli Mountains are 130 miles to the west of Stonehenge as the crow flies. To transport the Bluestones to the Plain would have involved an epic river raft journey, 240 miles from Wales, dragging the stones overland between the rivers. The route was around the Welsh Coast, up the Severn Estuary to the Bristol Channel, then along the rivers of southern England. In the thirteenth century the medieval city of New Sarum (Salisbury) was built in the meadows where five rivers meet; this was the final stage of the journey – along the

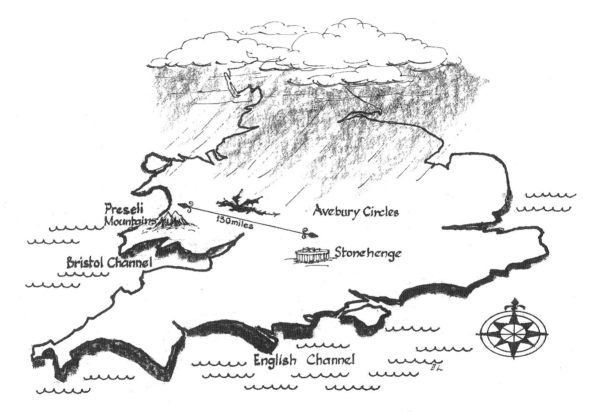

Preseli
Mountains

130 miles

Avebury Circles

Stonehenge

Bristol Channel

English Channel

Wiltshire Avon to what today is West Amesbury. The Bluestones would then have been pulled the last three miles across the landscape to the site.

The Beaker people dug a double circle of postholes but only erected three-quarters of the stones in a double flattened horseshoe shape. Either they ran out of stone or their vision of the sacred space they intended to create altered, The builders dismantled the Bluestones, reintroducing them later when all of the Sarsen stones were in place.

One of the Bluestones was carved with a groove down the side. Today it is leaning at an angle towards the fallen lintel of the greatest Trilithon at the heart of the monument. It is likely to have been one of a pair of stones, its companion having a tongue projection so that the stones fitted together in a male/female coupling position.

This Bluestone is unique on the site today. It may have been intended as a focal stone, representing the Goddess in an earlier monument, either in Wales or on the Plain, perhaps even at Stonehenge.

The Stranger Stones

The Sarsen stones began to arrive at approximately 2,200BC. The name is thought to have originated in the Middle Ages, the time of the Crusades. The Saracens were the strangers who lived in the Holy Land; the Sarsen stones were foreign to the Stonehenge landscape. The Sarsens came from twenty miles to the north, the area of the Marlborough Downs. Weighing up to fifty tonnes they were probably pulled across the rolling landscape on tree trunk rollers by men or by oxen. One estimate is that it would have taken a thousand men seven weeks in man-hours to move one stone to the site.

There were more than eighty Sarsens stones at Stonehenge; if each stone took 1,176 hours to transport, the total time commitment would have exceeded 94,080 hours.

The Sarsens are a type of sandstone with a very high surface resistance to abrasion, harder to work than steel.

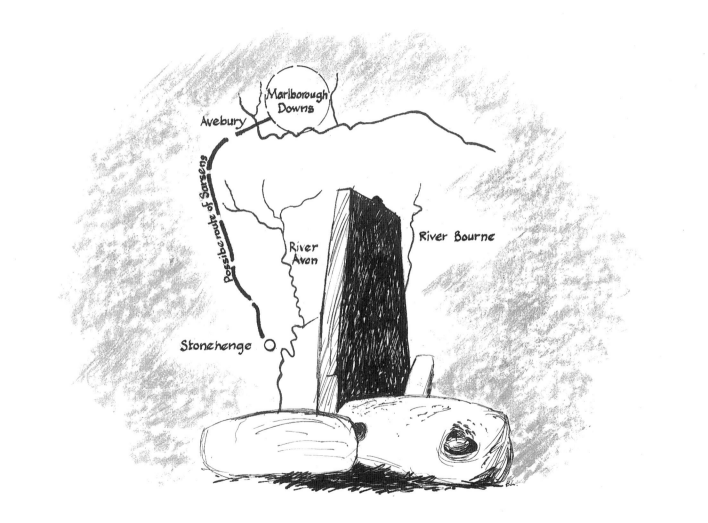

The inner circle is one of the earliest examples of a building we can still see – the beginnings of architecture, the prototype for temples and coliseums, unsurpassed in its originality. The only effective tools available to dress the hard sandstone more than four thousand years ago were Sarsen mauls with which the Beaker masons rubbed and hammered the stones into shape.

The outer Sarsen stones are neither dressed nor worked so are likely to be earlier than the circle itself. To one side of the main axis line stood a 35-ton stone that today inclines toward the circle and is called the Heel Stone. At the entrance to the henge bank were two or maybe three portal stones; the only one remaining today is the recumbent Slaughter Stone. Inside the circle of the henge bank and the Aubrey Holes, in the position of four corners of an invisible oblong, there were four Station Stones, two of which remain.

The effort it took to build Stonehenge offers a glimpse into the world of the Bronze Age Plainsmen. It tells us that they enjoyed a political and economic stability which allowed the great monument to be constructed over eight hundred years. In a landscape devoid of stones, the Bronze Age dynasties sought out exotic stones from far places. They spared manpower to collect the stones, proving that they must have lived during a halcyon time – they could not have allowed the strong young men to travel such distances if the tribes were likely to be at risk. The crops must have been plentiful to allow the builders to be spared from the fields, to be fed and taken care of by the rest of the community. Stonehenge stands as an eternal testament to the efficacy and favour of the Bronze Age Gods.

The Iron Age Shamen

There are two enduring facts about Stonehenge, both of which are wrong. The first is that the monument is a Druid Temple, the second that the summer solstice sunrise is directly over the Heelstone on the longest day.

The Druids were a Celtic Priesthood who did not exist

in history until the site had been abandoned for a thousand years. They were the leaders of a tribal society – the wise men, the Shamen of the Iron Age. The Druids were the healers, poets, genealogists, historians, storytellers, judges, priests and magicians with an oral tradition. They were a caste; men and women embraced the mysteries, retiring into deep caves and endless forests to study the lore of their ancestors. It has been suggested it would have taken them twenty years to accumulate the knowledge, which was in a form of verse.

The Druids were familiar with calendars and astronomy; they knew the lunar year took almost nineteen years to complete its cycle. They used the elements, fire and water in their sacred ceremonies, and ritual weapons for human and animal sacrifice to their gods. It is unlikely they would ever have worshipped at Stonehenge, the Druids did not worship in buildings but rather in groves of trees close to running water; the nearest river was three miles away at West Amesbury.

The Slaughter Stone was given its evocative name because it has iron ore deposits in the stone which leave red marks on the surface, especially when wet. Because of this and the fact that it is recumbent it was thought to be a bloodstained sacrificial stone used by the Druids in their rituals. It was one of either a pair or a trio of upright stones, an outer gateway to the site.

The confusion as to the builders began in the seventeenth century after the Civil War. The English were now too sophisticated to believe stone circles were built in the distant past by a mythical race of giants. Nor did they accept the medieval superstition that the stone circles were petrified humans who had angered the Gods, perhaps by dancing on the Sabbath, turned to stone and doomed to dance in a circle throughout eternity. The most obvious architects of the great stone circle were the Romans who had invaded Britain in 43AD and stayed for four centuries. When it was realised that Stonehenge was old and abandoned by the time Claudius's legions arrived, it was wrongly attributed to the Druids.

The Sun Stone

There are various explanations for the origin of the Heel Stones name. It was known as the Friar's Heel because on one side of the stone is an indentation like a footprint. Legend says the Devil, having magicked the stones from Ireland, built Stonehenge to puzzle and amaze mankind. He worked throughout the night, the darkness cloaking his activities. Early in the morning a friar came by and saw what the Devil was doing. Not unnaturally the man took to his heels. The Devil, furious to have been discovered, picked up the 35-ton Sarsen stone, threw it after the friar, hitting him on the foot. Because the friar was such a holy man God protected him, the indentation of the friar's foot was left on the stone, from then on it was known as the Heel stone.

Another origin for the name stems from *Helios*, the Greek word for the sun. Greek mythology tells of a great circular or elliptical temple in an island to the west dedicated to the sun god Apollo. The island has been identified as Britain, the Temple as Stonehenge. The summer solstice sunrise traditionally is over the Helios/Sunstone on the longest day, 21st June, when viewed from the centre of the monument. The earth's axis has altered slightly since Stonehenge was built; according to astronomers the midsummer sunrise has never been visible from the accepted position in the more than four thousand years since the Sarsen stones began to arrive. It will not be until the year 3,260 that the sun will rise over the Heelstone as seen from the centre of the circle.

Dr Meaden has two new explanations for the Heelstone's name in *Stonehenge: the Secret of the Solstice*. In the nineteenth century it was inferred that the Hele Stone came from the Anglo-Saxon word *helan* meaning to hide or conceal, suggesting it was a 'covering stone.'

Another more recent suggestion is that instead of 'the Friars Heel' the stone was called 'Freya's He-ol.' The ancient British/Nordic goddess Freya has the distinction of being the only female deity to have a day of the week named after her. *He-ol* is an old Welsh word for way or track. This would indicate that the Heelstone stood on the way or the path of the Goddess. Both these interpretations add credence to Dr. Meaden's conclusions that Stonehenge was a place for fertility rites and Mother Goddess worship.

The Unconquered Sun

In 1997 a brilliant comet returned to our vernal skies after a four thousand year orbit through the galaxy. Unromantically christened Hale Bopp, the last time the comet was visible from this planet the Sarsen stage of building was in progress on the Plain. The great circle at Stonehenge was built further before the birth of Christ than we are now after the event. As Christianity begins its third thousand years, Stonehenge enters its sixth millennium.

The Beaker people erected a Sarsen circle of thirty upright and thirty top stones. In the centre, in the shape of a horseshoe or the lowering horns of a bull, they raised five great Trilithons. Trilithon is from the Greek meaning three stones – two uprights with a lintel on the top, like five enormous doorways. The Trilithons graduated in height: the largest was at the back in the middle, framing the midwinter sunset.

For the Neolithic and Bronze Age farmers the midwinter festival must have had enormous significance. Throughout the summer, after the longest day of the summer solstice, imperceptibly but inevitably the Sky God, the Sun, begins to die. As the days become shorter, darkness envelops the winter landscape, the earth grows cold and infertile. It must have seemed as if their universe was about to be plunged into an eternal night, a place abandoned by warmth and light, where no crops would grow, where their animals would starve. They must have been terrified that their world was about to end.

The midwinter sunset, framed by the greatest Trilithon, heralded the Sun's rebirth. After the death throes of the

longest night, the God is reborn, the cycle of life renewed, the reincarnation of the earth begun. This belief system continued with the pagan fire festivals which evolved into medieval Christian celebrations.

November 1st was the Celtic festival of *Samhain* when bonfires were lit to ensure the sun's return after the winter. It was the time the sheep were mated and the annual slaughter of the surplus livestock took place. Once the harvest was in and the amount of fodder available was calculated, the number of animals to be kept through the winter could be assessed.

For both Christians and pagans November is associated with the cult of death. In the past it was believed to be a time when natural laws were suspended, a time the dead were unquiet, when ghosts and demons roamed abroad. Halloween on the 31st October, the eve of *Samhain*, still echoes this tradition and superstition. The early Christian Church rededicated 1st November All Saints day in 835. After the Gunpowder Plot of 1605 the emphasis of the fire festival changed; today, on 5th November, bonfires are lit and Guy Fawkes ceremonially burned across Britain. This autumnal fire ritual reaches back across at least two and a half thousand years in these islands, to a time before the Romans, a time of sacred groves, of mistletoe boughs, of the Druid priesthood and the Celtic peoples.

The midwinter solstice was when the pagans held their rites to honour the rebirth of the sun. When Pope Julius appropriated the day for the date of the birth of Jesus Christ in the fourth century he chose a day which had long been sacred. To the Romans December 25th was *Die Natalis Invicti Solis* – the birthday of the unconquered sun. From the Sun God to the Son of God, the merging of pagan and Christian beliefs were beginning.

The Midsummer Marriage

By 1,550BC the Bluestones had been reintroduced – a circle within the Sarsen Circle and a horseshoe of nineteen Bluestones within the Trilithon horseshoe.

Nineteen is an astronomical number, 18.61 solar years in a lunar year. The five Trilithons may have had astronomical significance, representing the five planets visible with the naked eye in the starry firmament: Mercury, Venus, Mars, Jupiter and Saturn.

At the focal point on the main axis line the Beaker builders placed a single unique stone. It was micaceous sandstone from the area of Milford Haven in Wales. This solitary monolith stood within the double circle and the double horseshoe of Sarsen and Bluestones. It was approximately twelve feet above the ground, standing at half the height of the great Trilithon behind it. It is commonly called the Altar Stone because, laying in the midst of the circle with the fallen lintel on top of it, the assumption was that it had been used as a pagan altar. It was an upright stone that faced the main entrance, the portal through which the summer solstice sun shone on the longest day. To the nature-worshipping, agricultural people it could have represented the Goddess or been a marker for the centre of their world.

Dr Meaden believes that Stonehenge was used as a fertility temple. In some cultures, including modern India, the Trilithon is seen as the entrance to the Earth Mother, at Stonehenge the outer circle of thirty upright and thirty top stones could be said to reinforce the message that this was a place of Goddess worship. The importance of the sexual act between the God and the Goddess to ensure the continuation of the life cycle is undisputed. The five Trilithons in the horseshoe are likened to the womb or the uterus of the Mother Goddess.

As the midsummer sun rose over the horizon it entered the monument through the main entrance, the vagina of the Earth Mother. As the first of the sun's rays fell upon the Goddess stone, the mica within the stone reacted to the light and sparkled with an incandescent magic. The Sky God and the Earth Goddess united in a sacred marriage. Then the sun touched the Heel/Helios stone, sending the phallic shadow of the megalith across the

landscape, penetrating the entrance into the sheltering womb, covering the Goddess stone in a second sexual act to ensure the fertility of the earth for the coming year. The imagery of the Midsummer marriage of the Gods, the union of the sky and the earth, of male and female deities, is compelling.

The Sarsen stones within the circle have been worked with carpentry techniques. The thirty lintels of the outer circle are joined horizontally with tongue and groove joints; the Sarsen uprights have vertical tenons on top and mortice holes under the lintels. These are basic woodworking joints and the builders may have been repeating techniques used in their wooden structures. The joints were unnecessary for the purpose of holding the stones in place; their weight ensured their stability. The tongue and groove and the mortice and tenon joints at Stonehenge are carpentry joints in stone; they are also reminiscent of male penetration during the sexual act.

The Goddess Precinct

On the inner face of one of the uprights of the fourth Trilithon there is a carving said to resemble the Neolithic Mother Goddess images found in the stone burial chambers of Brittany. Deciphering the carving is very difficult for the uninitiated and in most lights it is impossible to recognise. In this area the female influence is strong. The grooved Bluestone, its tongued companion long since vanished, inclines towards the centre. Opposite the carving, half buried in the chalk, lies the Goddess stone. It is fitting that the fallen lintel of the Trilithon archway covers this micaceous stone. The Bride stone of the Midsummer Marriage reclines across the portal that framed the reincarnation of her bridegroom, the Sun, at midwinter. This could be claimed as the Goddess precinct at Stonehenge.

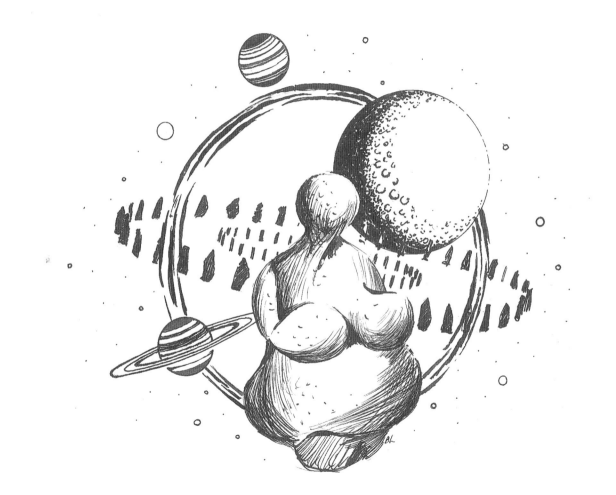

The Dragon Path

The Serpent and the Dragon

To past civilisations the serpent and the dragon were symbols of wisdom and holiness linked with the mystic and the spiritual world. The serpent was frequently associated with Goddess figures; it was a universal symbol of rebirth, perhaps because of the snake's ability to shed its skin and renew itself.

In 1926, at Faardal in Jutland, the richest late Bronze Age hoard in Denmark was discovered totally by chance. The jewellery and figurines date from between 900-700BC and among these treasures a pregnant mother goddess, right arm upraised, was found with a curved dragon figure, its coils imitating the pendulous breasts of the goddess. The goddess and the dragon could be joined together by placing the dragon's mouth into a hole in the hand of the goddess. There were three other dragon figures in the collection, now in the safe keeping of the Danish National Museum.

Many churches have pre-Christian images in their fabric, eg. the nature god of fertility known as the Green Man; the Sheela-na-gig, a blatantly sexual mother goddess figure; the dragon and the serpent, both of which featured in pagan and Christian worship. Salisbury Cathedral has various pagan carvings. The fifteenth century vaulted ceiling above the crossing has roof bosses decorated with foliage and a single head of a Green Man. Mid-thirteenth century bosses depicting dragons can be found within the building. A lone dragon, its wings folded, is perched on large leaves high above the north aisle, while in the cloisters is a keystone carved in a complex pattern and two winged dragons, apparently sinking their jaws into the skulls of a pair of horridly grimacing gargoyles.

At Avebury in Wiltshire the small church of St. James has a Norman font decorated with two serpents, their tails twisted, their open mouths turned towards a bishop holding a crozier. In Cornwall, Lostwithiel church font features both a Green Man and a grotesque gargoyle, the latter with serpents coiled across its head. In the Worcestershire village of Chaddesley Corbett the twelfth century font has a motif of bread like plaits on its rim and base. Around the bowl, dragons with entwining tails continue the intricate plaiting theme of the decoration. At East Haddon in Northamptonshire a circular font frieze from the thirteenth century is carved with foliage trails and a man holding two dragons.

Ireland, a country said to be completely devoid of snakes, associates with serpents more than any other country in Europe. Several Irish scholars see a close connection between solar, phallic and serpent worship. Many view the story of St. Patrick casting the snakes out of Ireland as a metaphor for the banishment of the pagan people and their old wisdom.

The dragon evolved from the serpent, initially having two front legs and a tail. Commonly called a wyvern, over the centuries it became a four-legged, fire-breathing

creature. Sacred sites around the world are likely to have an affinity with both creatures. The Minoan Palace of Knossos in Crete, which dates back to 2,000BC, has an area dedicated to the Mother Goddess. This female deity may have been known as Our Lady of the Labyrinth, the *labrys* was a double axe, the most sacred symbol in the Minoan religion

The Goddess cult at Knossos was powerful. The remains of a colossal Goddess statue approximately six foot high and two Snake Goddess figures made of fine glazed painted pottery known as faience were found in separate locations within the temple. The most famous of the Goddess figures is bare-breasted with twin serpents in each of her outstretched hands and is said to date from 1,600BC.

At Stonehenge there is a dagger carving from the period when the Mycenaean culture was flourishing, around 1,500BC. The second Trilithon has the Mycenaean-type dagger flanked by two axe heads on its closest upright to the main entrance. It faces the Trilithon with the Mother Goddess carving on the opposite side of the Sarsen horseshoe.

The Greek Temple of Delphi was a place where the Sun God Apollo and the Earth Mother were worshipped. The Oracle was a priestess who had the gift of prophecy and second sight when in a trance. The first Oracle was Sibylla or the Sibyl, the last was known as Pythia or the Pythoness, it was she who announced the death of the Sun God Apollo as Christianity began to triumph over the old Gods. By tapping into the earth energy, breathing vapours through a crevice, the Oracle would become a channel for the mysteries and the voice of the Gods, consulted by the heroes of Greek mythology. Alexander the Great is reputed to have visited Delphi for this purpose. He detoured to the site while en route to Macedonia in order to consult on the outcome of his Persian Crusade. Arriving sometime between late November and mid-February, the period when the Oracle

did not function, he forced himself into the presence of the priestess Pythia. She prophesied that Alexander was invincible, thus setting the seal of approval for his forthcoming campaign.

One of the Greek creation myths has the great serpent Ophion mating with Eurynome, the Goddess of All Things, as she emerges naked from Chaos. From this union came all life – all living creatures in the sky and on the earth were the result of the sexual act between the Goddess and the Serpent.

The Caduceus, a winged staff entwined with twin serpents, has a history which reaches across continents into Greek, Roman, Jewish and Egyptian tradition. In the Old Testament, during the exodus from Egypt to the Promised Land, the children of Israel turned from Jehovah. As a punishment He sent a plague of poisoned serpents which attacked the Israelites, killing many with their venom. After the people repented Jehovah told Moses to fashion a fiery serpent and set it on a pole, promising that all who looked upon it would be saved.

The Caduceus was a symbol used by heralds and ambassadors in the ancient world. Associated with the messengers of the Gods – Hermes to the Greeks and Mercury to the Romans – it was originally either a willow wand or an olive branch, hung with ribbons or garlands. Later, the twisted ribbons became two coiled serpents facing each other beneath a pair of wings.

The Greek God of healing, Asclepios, carried a Caduceus with a single snake upon it. Today the Caduceus is a worldwide emblem of the medical profession. The image of a dragon or a serpent eating its own tail, thus creating an endless life cycle, is a symbol of alchemy. The eternal circle, a compelling image, having no beginning and no end, absorbing and renewing itself just as the natural seasons and the life-giving waters of the oceans and rivers effortlessly merge and blend into each other.

In Egypt, cobra like serpents are coiled around the

head-dresses of the Pharaohs and the Gods, and are painted on the walls of the burial chambers. The dragons of the Creator God Marduk were part of the decoration of the Ishtar gate, named for the Goddess of love and war, and of the walls of the Ceremonial Way into Babylon around the sixth century BC.

Serpent symbolism is widespread across the Americas. The double-headed serpent was associated with rain, the water of life. It was used in the rituals of the bloodthirsty Aztec God Tlaloc, and in the ceremonies of the Hopi Indians of the American South-West. The Hopi, the Peaceful People, were descendents of the Anasazi, the Ancient Ones, pueblo dwellers and sun worshippers. During their religious rites the Hopi perform a snake dance for rain making; this involves dancing with snakes in their mouths.

In Ohio, sometime during the 2nd/1st century BC, the Hopewell Indians built a great Serpent Mound, an earthwork constructed in the shape of a snake. The mound, probably used for religious purposes, was 1,330 feet long, 19 feet across and 4 feet high.

Among the tribal legends of Mexico is the story of a white-bearded God who visited their ancestors bringing religion, culture and civilisation. The God has various local names: to the Aztecs he was Quetzalcoatl while the Mayans called him Kulkulkan, both names translate as the plumed or the feathered serpent. Quetzalcoatl was said to have returned across the sea from which he had come on a raft of serpents, promising to return.

At the time of the spring equinox the shadow serpent descends the steps of the pyramid of Kulkulkan, the Temple of the Sun, at Chichen Itza. As the sun begins to set, the celestial diamond-backed serpent gradually winds its way along the side of the north stairway from the sky towards the earth, a creature of sunlight amid encroaching darkness. The feathered rattlesnake is a manifestation of the God of both the Inca and the Mayan peoples, the serpent's descent a reaffirmation of the

continuation of life after death.

The Burning Dragon

Dragons have been symbols of power through recorded history. In the language of heraldry the dragon is a sign for triumph over tyranny. The dragon standard originated in Britain with the Roman cohorts, arriving in the first four centuries after Christ. A cohort, one tenth of a Roman legion, was made up of six centuries or companies of eighty men.

According to medieval tradition the standard was reputed to have been used by the Pendragon dynasty in the fifth century. Dragons were also common on the war banners of the Celts, the Anglo-Saxons and the Germanic tribes.

The beginning of the Welsh identification as the land of the Red Dragon comes from Celtic Arthurian lore. King Vortigen attempted to build a great fortress beneath Mount Snowdon. Each day the workmen would labour and each night the work would mysteriously be undone.

Vortigen consulted his magicians who claimed that he should sacrifice a fatherless child and sprinkle his blood on the foundations. A young boy – some legends say he was named Ambrosius, others that this was King Arthur's arch-druid Merlin – revealed that beneath the site dwelt two dragons, and that each night the dragons fought, undermining the foundations of the building. The boy was able to see a hidden lake where the two dragons, one white, one red, slept. The dragons awoke and fought ferociously until the red dragon was victorious. The child said that the red dragon represented the Britons while the white dragon symbolised the invaders from across the sea. The native Britons were living mainly in the west and the north of the country. It was not until the middle of the seventh century that the Welsh established a separate identity.

The first documented evidence of the red dragon comes from an ancient text; the 'gorchan of Maeldderw' dated around 600. The heraldic symbol of the burning dragon related to Cadwaladr, the hero expected to deliver the Welsh from the English according to prophecy. Cadwaladr was the son of Cadwallon ap Cadfan, a seventh century King of Gwynedd. Cadwallon was the only British King to overthrow an English dynasty. When the warrior King Edwin of Northumbria invaded Wales, Cadwallon, allied with Penda of Mercia, fulfilled Merlin's prophetic utterance, the victory of the red dragon over the white, by defeating Edwin at the battle of Haethfelth in 632.

The West Saxons adopted the golden dragon, which became the symbol of Wessex. The standard was carried by a succession of English Kings, including the last Anglo-Saxon King, Harold Godwinsson, killed at the Battle of Hastings by the invading Normans in 1066.

The dragon reappears with the fiery red dragon standard of Henry Tudor at the Battle of Bosworth Field in 1485. This was the final battle of the Wars of the Roses, the conflict between the dynasties of York and Lancaster. By adopting the red dragon of Cadwaladr,

Henry VII sought to establish his royal bloodline as a descendent of the last native ruler of Britain. He also introduced a pendant of St George and the Dragon to the collar of the Order of the Garter, established during the reign of Edward III in the mid-fourteenth century.

Elizabeth I was the last English sovereign to have the Tudor Dragon on the Royal Coat of Arms. When she died without heirs in 1603 James I, the son of Mary Queen of Scots and Lord Darnley, succeeded her. The Stuart dynasty ruled for just over a century, with a brief interruption after the English Civil War. Between 1649-1660 the Welsh Dragon was reinstated in the arms of the Commonwealth, also known as the Interregnum, replacing the Scottish Unicorn and its association with the executed Stuart King, Charles I.

The Pendragon Legacy

The whole area around Stonehenge is steeped in ancient tales that are interwoven with Arthurian legend. *Ambresbury* (Amesbury) was an important religious

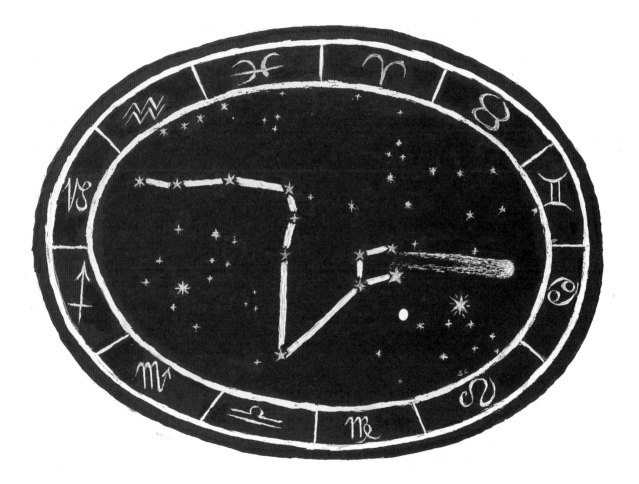

centre beside the river *Afon* (Avon). It was named after one of King Arthur's uncles, Aurelius Ambrosius. Arthur's father Uther succeeded Ambrosius as King of Britain. The death of Ambrosius was revealed to Merlin when he saw a brilliant star in the sky, its comet tail of light forming a dragon with two rays radiating from its open mouth. It was a portent that Uther was now the King and that a powerful son would follow him.

The Welsh bards described the bravery of their leaders using dragon similes; in old and middle Welsh and throughout the medieval period, dragon, *draig* or *dragwn* could mean either dragon, warrior, hero, chieftain or war leader, while *pen* meant head. Uther took the name of Pendragon (Dragon's Head), hence the title 'head dragon' or 'chief leader.'

Sometime early in the fifth century, following the Roman Occupation, a Welsh noble of the Gewissei tribe became a High King in the region. Vortigen the Thin was probably an 'over chief' of a group of tribal chieftains.

His wife Renwein was the daughter of Hengist, an infamous Saxon invader. Hengist called a May Day meeting at Amesbury to discuss a peace treaty between the Saxons and the Britons. After feasting, the Saxons pulled daggers from their boots and slaughtered 460 of the unarmed British nobles. The murdered nobles were buried on Salisbury Plain and Aurelius Ambrosius erected a worthy monument, Stonehenge, as their memorial. The stones came from Ireland, magicked to the plain by Merlin, the Druid magician. Some stories say they came by air, some by sea and some that the Devil brought them.

Both the Stonehenge Bluestones and the Sarsens have connections with the Welsh enchanter of Arthurian mythology. Merlin, from the Latin *Merlinus* and the Welsh *Myrddin*, came from the land of the Dragon, born in Carmarthen not far from the place of the Bluestones, the Preseli Mountains of Wales. His reputed burial mound, Merlin's Mount, is at Marlborough, close to the Avebury landscape, the source of the Sarsen stones. The

Avebury

Silbury
Hill

Avebury Sanctuary is a great Serpent Temple built of unworked local Sarsen stones that are scattered across the Marlborough Downs. It is a place of Dragon Power, of Mother Goddess worship, where the sacred mysteries and fertility rituals were celebrated for countless generations.

One of the possible locations for Camlann, King Arthur's final battle, is Salisbury Plain. When Arthur's illegitimate son Mordred attempted to usurp the throne, the warring factions gathered for a final confrontation at daybreak. The night before the battle King Arthur dreamed that he should wait for Sir Lancelot, who was on his way with reinforcements, and that he would die if he fought Mordred the next day. In the morning Arthur called a meeting to arrange a truce. Both sides sent a delegation of knights. As the two groups converged a viper stung one of the knights who, in drawing his sword, precipitated the battle.

Throughout the long day the armies fought. Despite

massive casualties the eventual victory was Arthur's. Disregarding his premonition, Arthur fought and killed Mordred in hand-to-hand combat. In his death throes Mordred pierced Arthur's helmet, his sword penetrating the Kings brain and fatally wounding him.

It was in Amesbury Abbey that Queen Guinevere had sought seclusion when her adulterous love affair with Sir Lancelot was discovered. It was there she heard the news of her widowhood from Lancelot, who had arrived too late to save the King. She took the veil as a penance after her husband's death. She died at Amesbury and her lover Lancelot escorted her horse-drawn bier from there to Glastonbury for burial.

A tomb, said to be of the fabled King and Queen, was unearthed in 1191. It was a Celtic burial, the bones of a man and a woman in a hollow oak between two stone pyramids. Inside the grave was a leaden cross with an inscription bearing King Arthur's name. It was a very providential discovery; a fire in 1184 had decimated most of the old Abbey buildings. At first, financial aid was forthcoming from many sources, including the Angevin King, Henry II.` When Henry died his son Richard I (the Lionheart) was more interested in financing the Crusades than restoring Glastonbury Abbey. The need for benefactors and pilgrims to continue to donate generously was urgent, the grave of the once and future King and his consort proved a magnet to the medieval world, ensuring the prosperity of the Abbey.

The story of King Arthur that we recognise today originated in the first half of the thirteenth century when Geoffrey of Monmouth wrote his *History of the Kings of Britain*. Historical information is scanty and so entangled with legend that it is difficult to unravel fact from fiction. The oral tradition for the existence of Arthur stretches back into Dark Age Celtic lore. An ancient Welsh poem of around 600 tells of a great battle between Saxon and British forces, comparing one of the warriors to Arthur. The *Historia Brittonum*, written at the very beginning of the ninth century, gives a similar account and the tenth century *Annals of Wales* refers to Arthur's battles, his victory at Badon and to his death twenty-one years later at the battle of Camlann.

Arthur seems to be a figure of the 460s, possibly based on Riothamus, a British chieftain who disappears from the records in 470 in Gaul. Riothamus could have been a title rather than a name, a 'high king' of Britain. After the Roman legions left the indigenous people, British and Romano-British became independent and were initially successful in fighting off invaders. In 468 Riothamus sailed to Gaul at the head of his army to fight the Visigoths in support of the Roman Empire. After being defeated in battle Riothamus escaped with a handful of loyal companions. This is the last documented evidence of his existence. He disappears from history as completely as Arthur vanishes from mythology.

The Chinese Dragon

Before the Henge appeared in prehistory the Chinese were practising acupuncture. This recognises two opposite and complimentary energies flowing along pathways known as meridians. The ancient Chinese people called the energy "the Dragon Power" and the energy lines "the Dragon Paths." Today the energy lines are known as ley lines and the Dragon power is referred to as earth energy, earth forces or earth magic.

The art of Feng-Shui, literally translated as wind-water, refers to the earth energy as "ch'i", "cosmic or dragons breath." Feng-Shui is a system of balance and harmony, working with the natural world, going with rather than against the flow. It recognises positive and negative energy, choosing the most favourable site for objects or buildings.

If one thinks of the "mother" earth as a living entity, coursing through the planet the life force, veins of energy, which the peoples of the past could instinctively, recognise. Stone pillars, placed on earthly power points are said to act as acupuncture needles, penetrating the veins of the dragon, the core of energy, channelling and strengthening strong earth places.

Earth magic is frequently misunderstood. The force appears to be a natural phenomenon as yet unknown. Electricity, radio, television, microwaves, are just a few modern discoveries, which would have been seen as witchcraft in previous centuries.

The Paths of Power

The old Saxon words *leye* and *ley*, alternative spellings *lea*, *lee* or *leigh*, have different meanings. *Leye* meant fire or flame, often referred to in place names as a beacon fire, while *ley* was defined as 'a field temporarily under grass' or 'a tract of open land'.

The first person to use the term as we think of it today was Alfred Watkins in *The Old Straight Track*. The book, first published in 1925, is still in print today. Alfred Watkins lived in Hereford; when he left school he became an outrider or brewer's representative, travelling widely in his native countryside around the Welsh borders.

Watkins noticed that traditionally sacred sites such as burial mounds, standing stones, earthworks, beacon hills and churches built on the earlier pagan sites seemed to be arranged in straight lines. His original interpretation was that these were prehistoric sight lines across the landscape; today we think of them as earth energy paths.

Stonehenge is the focal point of a sacred and a ritual landscape. The monument is like the hub of a wheel; radiating out, like the spokes of the wheel, are lines of energy, the most powerful alignment being the main axis line through the site.

The builders of the henge and the rings of stone were attuned to the natural world. Certain peoples such as the American Indians, the Bushmen of the Kalahari and the Australian Aboriginals live in touch with their environment and with nature. In the same way that old sailors can feel a storm brewing, that some countrymen can predict a frost and that animals can sense an impending earthquake, I believe the architects of Stonehenge and of mystic sites around the world recognised the power points of the earth.

The energy has yet to be measured scientifically, it is not recognisably magnetic but it can as easily be detected by pendulums, or by using dowsing rods of wood or plastic as of metal. Children often say they feel odd, tingling sensations on the lines. Some people are particularly sensitive – psychics and healers frequently sense the power. The energy is transmitted through the human body which acts as a conductor. It is possible that the builders of Stonehenge and other sacred sites such as the pyramids of Egypt, Mexico and South America knew how to utilise the power in a way that we have long since forgotten. This would explain the complex astronomical observations of ancient civilisations. Many mystic sites appear to be venerated as places of healing; at Stonehenge it is said if one washes in the charged water that has touched the stones it has healing properties.

The Dragon at Stonehenge

Earth energy places are often associated with dragons or serpents; one of the Stonehenge legends suggests it was a temple of dragon or serpent worship. The longest and most famous ley line in Britain is the St. Michael line, along whose length there are recurrent locations connected with dragon legends. The line, beginning in the west at Land's End and ending in the North Sea near Lowestoft in Suffolk, passes through many churches dedicated to St. Michael or St. George, both dragon slaying saints.

Stonehenge has two famous 'dragon paths' – the Stonehenge Ley and the Old Sarum Ley. The Stonehenge line is 22 miles long running from the south-west to the north-east. The alignment travels from Castle ditches, through a dewpond, Grovely Castle, a bell barrow at Normington Down, Stonehenge and the Avenue, Sidbury

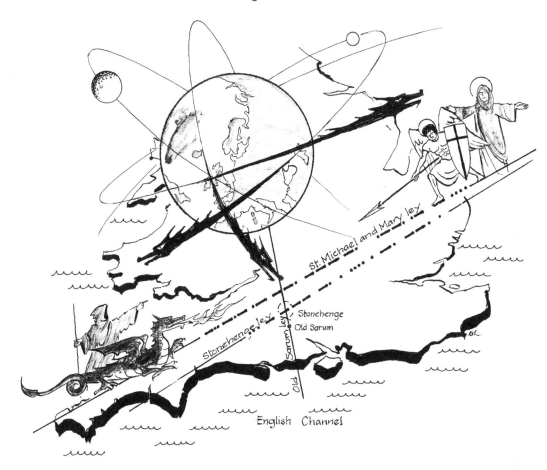

St. Michael and Mary ley

Stonehenge ley

Old Sarum ley

Stonehenge
Old Sarum

English Channel

Camp and two more burial mounds. At Stonehenge the ley line runs close to the Midsummer sunrise alignment, the Solstice path of the Sky God to the Bride stone.

The 18-mile Old Sarum Ley begins at the pregnant Earth Goddess mound, the largest round barrow in the area, the Monarch of the Plain. It is close to Dr Meaden's tornado path, the place of sexual union between the deities, the Cursus monument. It penetrates the Henge bank, on to Old Sarum, Salisbury Cathedral, Clearbury Ring and Frankenbury Camp.

Old Sarum is an Iron Age hill fort built somewhere between 600BC and 43AD when the Romans invaded Britain. It was in use during the Dark Ages and had strategic importance in the West Country throughout recorded history. After the Norman Conquest in 1066 a castle was built atop a new earth mound in the centre of the Iron Age defences. Four years later, in 1070, having successfully subdued resistance, William the Conqueror disbanded his troops at Old Sarum. The first cathedral

was built by the end of the eleventh century and a thriving city encompassed the great stone castle.

By 1215 the windswept site had become untenable. The town was overcrowded and there was no longer any space to build within the fortifications, the clergy and townspeople were constantly in conflict with the garrison and the main water source was in the castle so the price was controlled by the military. It was agreed the cathedral should relocate; in order to decide where it should be sited legend says that an archer with a longbow stood at the top of the castle ramparts and that wherever his arrow struck would mark the site of the new cathedral. The arrow travelled two miles – this has been explained away by suggesting that the arrow wounded a deer, the deer ran on, eventually expiring in a field owned by the Bishop. Another conjecture is that the arrow was in fact a constellation known as the Arrow of Apollo.

The route of the arrow follows the dragon path, finding its way to Myrfield, the meadow named for the Virgin

Mary. It is likely that in the medieval world the ancient knowledge was still available. To admit to belief was to risk being accused of heresy, so the arrow story was adopted. Salisbury Cathedral is built on an energy point. The confluence of five rivers make the location a recognisable dragon place, with the Cathedral protectively embraced by the river Avon. The building, its spire and tower weighing 6,400 tonnes, is built on shingly shale, so its foundations are only four feet deep. For almost eight hundred years this exquisite example of Early English Gothic architecture has stood on an unstable surface.

When Christianity arrived in Britain during the Roman Occupation it co-existed with the old gods. The Romans were remarkably tolerant of religious belief; they brought their deities with them but respected the local gods. Jesus Christ was worshipped alongside the Sky God, the Earth Goddess and the Roman Emperors. Early in the fifth century the Roman Empire began to decline, the

legions returned to their homeland and left Britain to the invasions of the Jutes, Angles and Saxons. The Christian Church retreated westwards into the Celtic lands: the Welsh mountains, the wild moors of Cornwall and across the sea to Ireland and to Brittany.

The seventh century was the period when Christianity began to spread the length and breadth of Britain. Between 634 and 650 a Roman missionary named Birinus brought the Christian message to Wessex, the land of the West Saxons and the place of the great pagan temple, Stonehenge.

Gradually the period of religious absorption began. Christian churches were built on sites that had long been sacred, the people forced into the new buildings to access the Dragon points. The Mother Goddess and Sun God worship continued. The male dominated Catholic Church encouraged reverence for the Virgin Mary, the Mother Goddess gradually becoming embodied within the person of the Mother of Christ.

By adopting the midwinter date of the Roman *Die Natalis Invicti Solis* and the pagan rebirth of the Sun God for the celebration of Christ's birth, Pope Julius successfully dispossessed the pagans once more. Eventually the new God would become all-powerful and the old belief system would no longer be conciously remembered.

The new churches erected on earth energy points were the power places recognised by earlier generations. Thus the unification of the belief system had ensured, though the ideology had been transformed, the Dragon power remained as it always had been, at the centre of human worship. Christian churches were built on pagan sites, the Virgin Mary absorbing the Mother Goddess, and the rebirth of the Sun God was now identified as the nativity of the Son of God.

The Language of the Stones

Journalist Richard le Gallienne (1866-1947) described the great stone circle in *Travels in England* published in

1900. He wrote, 'And Stonehenge, I remembered, had given me an unforgettable thrill of mystery, though that stone writing upon the green page of Salisbury Plain was in a language I could not read. But the shape of the letters alone fascinated me-and, indeed, it is not merely fanciful to say that at a distance Stonehenge is not unlike a Hebrew inscription written in stone.'

Le Gallienne had perfectly described the awe and wonder which Stonehenge evokes. In Hebrew the Trilithon symbol represents the word *chi* meaning life. To the Jews life is sacrosanct, the physical life in this world a preparation for the spiritual life after death. *Chi* refers to the present physical life. The symbol can be traced back through Jewish texts three and a half thousand years, to around 1,500BC, the period of the abandonment of Stonehenge.

Within the Jewish faith the name of God is so sacred He is only spoken of indirectly. *Adonai* meaning 'My Lord' is used by believing Jews; *Yahweh, Jehovah, Elohim* are

forbidden as personal names capture the essence or spirit. Both the ciphers for *Hashem* which translates to 'the Name', one of the ways of referring to God, and Jehovah use the Trilithon symbol.

The outer ring at Stonehenge is made up of thirty uprights and thirty lintels, the Trilithon horseshoe consisting of five towering doorways. Thus the external circle of Sarsen stones and the internal Trilithons could be said to be the trinity of fertility – the creation of life, the name of God and the womb of the Goddess.

Omega

The Welsh have a word, *hiraeth*, meaning a longing, a yearning for their homeland.

For as long as mankind exists Stonehenge will continue to exert an irresistible universal sense of hiraeth for unborn generations. It acts as a magnet and a mirror, a sacred space for the key moments of countless lifetimes, the act of creation, spiritual longing, ancestor worship, death and reincarnation.

As the world moves ever further from the Stonehenge people, the monument remains an eternal enigma, with secrets that can never be unlocked. It will always be the temple at the dawn of time, a place to touch the soul and stir the imagination, reflecting the heartbeat of the planet and the rhythm of the changing seasons. Amid the silent stones the old God's walk, echoes of past mysteries elude our consciousness, tantalisingly just beyond our reach.

At Stonehenge the pillars of stone tap into the life force of the planet, the Dragon Paths radiate across the sacred landscape. As the world revolves in its infinite orbit through space, at Stonehenge the Earth Goddess, the Sky God and the Dragon Power remain integral to the eternal cycle of regeneration and rebirth.

Romy Wyeth
In the year of the Dragon
August 2000

Acknowledgements

I would like to thank all those who were so patient with me and helped in the research of this book, especially Justin Bradbury who explained the Hebrew alphabet and the meaning of the words at length and often, to Terence Meaden for encouraging me to explore the world of the Mother Goddess and to Julie Gardiner for allowing me to check archaeological facts. I am very grateful to all those who tracked down obscure details, the Salisbury District Librarian Bruce Purvis who found out about the caduceus, dragon fonts and symbolism, Iwan ap Dafydd and Gareth England of the National Library of Wales for a wealth of Welsh information, to the Chief Librarian at the London Centre for Hebrew Studies for his insight into Jewish customs. Thanks to Dr Birger Storgaard of the Royal Society of Northern Antiquaries for telling me about the Jutland hoard and the Faardal Goddess, to Julian Noyce for finding Alexander the Great at Delphi, to Rev. Ian Duff for help with early Christianity in Wessex and to Kiran Poolman for origins and mythology surrounding the Cadudeus. Finally, to the man without whose brilliant illustrations *The Dragon Path* would not have been possible, Brian Lewis.

Bibliography

The following books contain further information on the subjects covered in *The Dragon Path and the Goddess*:

Deveraux, Paul: *The New Ley Hunters Guide*. Gothic Image, 1994.

Graves, Robert: *Greek Myths*. Cassell, 1981.

Graves, Tom: *Needles of Stone Revisited*. Gothic Image, 1986.

Lofmark, Carl: *A History of the Red Dragon*. Carreg & Gwalch, 1995.

Meaden, Terence: *The Secret of the Solstice*. Souvenir Press, 1997.

Miller, Hamish & Bradhurst, Paul: *The Sun and the Serpent*. Pendragon Press, 1989.

Watkins, Alfred: *The Old Straight Track*. Abacus, 1987.